Water Wise

WHAT ABOUT DROUGHTS?

Gail Parman

PowerKiDS press

Published in 2027 by
The Rosen Publishing Group, Inc.
2544 Clinton Street, Buffalo, NY 14224

Designer: Beeline Media and Design
Editor: Tricia Hoffman

Portions of this work were originally authored by Michael Rajczak and published as *Where's the Water?: Deadly Droughts*. All new material in this edition is authored by Gail Parman.

Photo credits: Cover, p. 1 Piyaset/Shutterstock.com; cover, p. 1 SaltyArts Design/Shutterstock.com; cover, p. 1, 4, 6, 8, 10, 12, 14, 16, 18, 20, 21, 24 (wave) vectorstuff/Shutterstock.com; p. 4 New Africa/Shutterstock.com; p. 5 Lisaopreis/Shutterstock.com; p. 6 ARTONIUMW/Shutterstock.com; p. 7 NOAA; p. 9 Goldilock Project/Shutterstock.com; p. 11 Najib elmaallem/Shutterstock.com; p. 13 Ververidis Vasilis/Shutterstock.com; p. 15 Victoria Ditkovsky/Shutterstock.com; p. 17 Spill The Tea Photography/Shutterstock.com; p. 18 Magic Lens/Shutterstock.com; p. 19 Mark Roberts Films/Shutterstock.com; p. 20 BubbleTeaOriginal/Shutterstock.com; p. 21 Bokeh Blur Background/Shutterstock.com

Cataloging-in-Publication Data
Names: Parman, Gail.
Title: What about droughts? / Gail Parman.
Description: Buffalo, New York : PowerKids Press, 2027. | Series: Water wise | Includes glossary and index.
Identifiers: ISBN 9781499458374 (pbk.) | ISBN 9781499458381 (library bound) | ISBN 9781499458398 (ebook)
Subjects: LCSH: Droughts--Juvenile literature.
Classification: LCC QC929.25 P377 2027 | DDC 551.5773--dc23

Printed in China

CPSIA Compliance Information: Batch #QSPK27. For Further Information contact Rosen Publishing at 1-800-237-9932.

Contents

Dry Droughts

Just like people, plants can get thirsty. If plants go too long without water, they may wilt or turn brown. Sometimes, when there's no rain for a week or so during a hot summer, lawns may even stop growing. Watering your garden will help your plants look healthy again.

Periods of dry weather are natural. But what happens when there's little or no rain for many months or even years? A very long dry period like this is called a drought. Sometimes, droughts can cause big problems.

Go with the Flow

You have to water your garden carefully. Just wetting the surface soil isn't enough. Make sure there's enough water to reach down to the roots of the plants.

Droughts affect plants, but they impact animals and people too.
Every living thing on Earth needs water!

Declaring a Drought

Even if it hasn't rained for a while, that doesn't always mean there's a drought. A drought in one place may just be a short dry spell in another. A drought occurs when there is very little **precipitation** for a long time, usually a season or more.

Meteorologists at the National Weather Service (NWS) and the U.S. Department of Agriculture watch weather and soil conditions closely for signs of very dry conditions. Depending on the conditions, these government groups may officially **declare** a drought.

Go with the Flow

Some parts of the world have soil that holds water better than other places, making droughts happen less often.

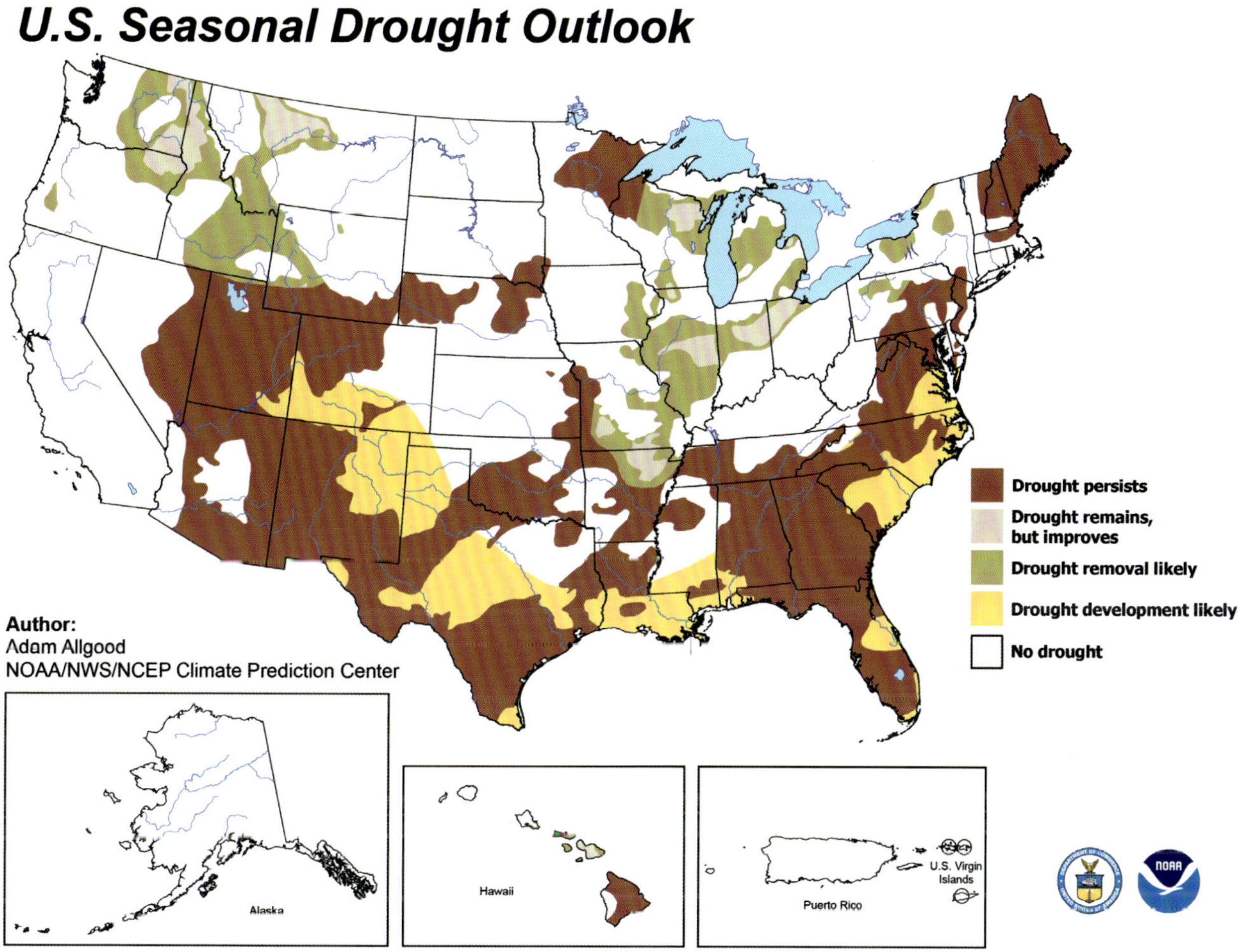

The NWS keeps track of precipitation amounts for the entire United States.

Meteorological Drought

There are three different kinds of droughts. When a place receives far less than the usual amount of rain for that area, it's called a meteorological drought.

For example, Buffalo, New York, usually gets just over 40 inches (102 cm) of rain each year. If only 20 inches (51 cm) fell, there would likely be drought conditions there. On the other hand, Phoenix, Arizona, usually gets just over 8 inches (20 cm) of rain a year. If it received 20 inches, that would be much more rain than usual—definitely not a drought!

Go with the Flow

The driest place in the United States is Death Valley in California. Over the past 50 years, Death Valley has received only about 2.3 inches (5.8 cm) of rainfall each year.

Not all places need the same amount of rain. It all depends on the regular conditions of an area.

Agricultural Drought

An agricultural drought is a shortage of water at different points in a plant's growth. After seeds are planted, they need lots of water. If there's not enough, plants may not grow. If some plants do grow, there will likely be far fewer than usual.

Later, when fruits begin to **develop**, plants need a lot of water again. If there's not enough, fewer fruits will grow. When there's an agricultural drought, people may have to pay more for fruits and vegetables because the need is greater than the supply. Droughts affect people in ways you may not have guessed!

Go with the Flow

Agricultural droughts happen because of too little precipitation. How well the soil holds on to moisture is also a big part of a drought like this happening.

Fruits that do develop during an agricultural drought will be smaller and may even taste different than usual.

Hydrological Drought

When there's a long period of dry weather, water levels in lakes, rivers, and even underground can drop. When this happens, it's called a hydrological drought.

Meteorological droughts can lead to hydrological droughts. When too little rain falls, not enough water seeps into the ground to keep groundwater levels steady. Groundwater is the water that exists beneath the Earth's surface. It helps fill rivers and lakes.

Low water levels can cause problems. People who use water from lakes and rivers in their homes may have to use less water. Dams that use water to create electricity may not be able to operate.

Go with the Flow

Hydrological droughts happen slowly. It can take many years for groundwater levels to fill back up.

Sometimes, low water levels harm fish and wildlife.

Using Too Much

Sometimes, people can cause water shortages too. This can happen if too many people begin to settle in a place that doesn't have enough water **resources**.

For example, many people visit Las Vegas, Nevada. The hotels there use over 3 billion gallons (11 billion L) of water every year! But the area around Las Vegas is a desert, because it receives just over 4 inches (10 cm) of rain each year. In a dry place like this, using so much water can cause a big water shortage. The hotels in Las Vegas must try to **conserve** water in any way possible.

Go with the Flow

When the need for water is greater than the supply of water, it's called a socioeconomic drought. This can happen because a new neighborhood was built or a farmer started planting more fields.

Even in an area that has had enough water over the years, an increase in the amount of water used can cause problems.

Dust Storms

During the 1930s, parts of Texas, Oklahoma, Kansas, Colorado, and New Mexico were hit with a long drought that lasted eight years! The area became so dry that it was known as the Dust Bowl.

Lack of rainfall helped cause this long drought, but farmers had also used the land poorly. The Great Plains had once been a large grassland, but farmers plowed too much of it. There were no plant roots for the soil to hold on to. Big windstorms blew the dry soil around. Thousands of acres of farmland lost all or most of their soil. Many people left their homes to escape the dust storms and all the damage they caused.

Go with the Flow

Where did all the soil go? Huge clouds of wind-driven soil flew hundreds of miles and even reached the East Coast!

Dust storms still happen today in places like Phoenix, Arizona.

Droughts Today

In December 2025, just over 35 percent of the United States was facing drought conditions. Many states in the western United States, including Arizona, Idaho, and Colorado, were part of the drought. These dry conditions made farming harder and led to an increase in wildfires. During droughts, dry land allows wildfires to spread quickly, which can harm homes, neighborhoods, and wildlife.

As **global climate change** continues, scientists say the droughts and the damage they cause could get even worse.

Go with the Flow
California had been in a drought for more than seven years! It officially ended in October 2023.

During a drought, people hope for snowstorms. Mountain snows melt in the springtime, filling **reservoirs** and increasing the amount of water in streams and lakes.

Conserving Water

Droughts can cause long-term harm to an area. Many cities and states have laws about how water is used, such as cleaning and reusing **wastewater**. When there's a drought, even more rules may come into effect. In 2015, California passed many rules about conserving water. One changed the kind of grass that could be grown on lawns, allowing only plants able to withstand drought conditions.

People can help prevent droughts, and that means you can help too! Simple changes can make a big difference.

Go with the Flow

We use the most water in our homes when we take a shower or flush the toilet.

You Can Help!

Turn off the water when you brush your teeth or wash your face. There's no need to keep the water running when you're not using it.

Take a shower instead of a bath. Short showers can keep you clean and save water too.

Ask your parents to fix a leaky sink, shower, or toilet. Leaks waste a lot of water.

Collect the water that you use to rinse fruits or vegetables. It can be reused to water plants or flush the toilet.

Use a bucket to collect rainwater. Use it to water your garden during dry spells.

Glossary

conserve: to keep something from harm and not waste it

declare: to make known publicly

develop: to grow and change

global climate change: long-term change in Earth's weather, caused partly by human activities such as burning oil and natural gas

meteorologist: someone who studies weather, climate, and the atmosphere

precipitation: rain, snow, sleet, or hail

reservoir: a place where something is stored

resource: a usable supply of something

wastewater: water that has been used

Fact Check

1. What is the driest place in the United States?
   a. Death Valley, California
   b. Phoenix, Arizona
   c. Las Vegas, Nevada

2. Agricultural droughts happen because of too little____________.
   a. climate change
   b. precipitation
   c. dust

3. Which of these activities uses the most water in our home?
   a. flushing the toilet
   b. brushing our teeth
   c. washing our face

Answers: 1. a, 2. b, 3. a

On the Internet

Drought for Kids
https://drought.unl.edu/Education/DroughtforKids.aspx
Learn more about what causes droughts and how they affect our lives.

Save Our Water
https://saveourwater.com/how-to-save-water/#1
How can you help in a drought? Find out here!

Publisher's note to educators and parents: Our editors have carefully reviewed these websites to ensure that they are suitable for students. Many websites change frequently, however, and we cannot guarantee that a site's future contents will continue to meet our high standards of quality and educational value. Be advised that students should be closely supervised whenever they access the Internet.

Index